GOODNIGHT BUSH

An Unauthorized Parody

by Erich Origen & Gan Golan

LITTLE, BROWN AND COMPANY

New York   Boston   London

In the situation room

There was a toy world

And a flight costume

And a picture of—

A refinery plume

And there were war profiteers giving three cheers

A nation great

A Church and a State

A pair of towers
And a balance of powers

A Grand Old Party to war in a rush

And a quiet Dick Cheney whispering "hush"

Goodnight refinery plume

Goodnight jets flying over the plume

Goodnight toy world
And the flight costume

Goodnight ballot box
Goodnight FOX

Goodnight towers

And goodnight balance of powers

Goodnight Constitution

And goodnight evolution

Goodnight democracy

And goodnight privacy

Goodnight old growth trees

Goodnight detainees

Goodnight allies

Goodnight Abu Ghraib "Cheese!"

Goodnight contractor beheading

Goodnight innocent bloodshedding

Goodnight nation great
And goodnight Church and State

Goodnight bubble bursting in air

And goodnight piggy beyond repair

Goodnight Rule of Law

And goodnight Mardi Gras

Goodnight Grand Old Party

Goodnight war in a rush

And goodnight to Dick Cheney whispering "hush"

Goodnight earth?

Goodnight heir?

Goodnight failures everywhere

Thank you!

We'd like to award the following people a Medal of Freedom: Lisa, Friedel, Yasmin, Ara, Mark, Jeff, Stephen, Janet, Cristie, Eric, David, Jodie, Benny, Emily, Kevin, Conan, Judy, Karen, Randal, Allyson, Eric, Gina, April, Bob, Mark, Stephani, Rich, Matthew, Yvonne, Chuck, Marie, Eli, William, Freddie, Linda, Christine, Joe, Jon, Rick, Sherrod and of course Margaret and Clement.

Afterword

In 1946, George W. Bush was born; one year later, *Goodnight Moon* was first published. The toddler classic and the future president have been inseparable ever since. Go to the White House website, and you'll find that Laura Bush placed *Goodnight Moon* first on her list of books to read to and with young children. Her brother-in-law, former Florida governor Jeb Bush, has called *Goodnight Moon* one of his favorite books from childhood. During President Bush's first term, the traditional Christmas gingerbread White House included a room made to look precisely like the one in *Goodnight Moon*. Bush himself, while campaigning, referred to *Goodnight Moon* as one of his childhood favorites (along with Eric Carle's *The Very Hungry Caterpillar*, which was not actually published until one year after Bush graduated from college; the president's infancy was clearly an extended one).

Why the affinity? The Bush family is certainly not alone: since its publication, *Goodnight Moon* has sold more than eleven million copies and become one of the most influential children's books of all time. And yet, there is more to it than that. When we were children nodding off to *Goodnight Moon* night after night, how could we have known that by reading Margaret Wise Brown and Clement Hurd's classic we were being conditioned for the forthcoming Bush administration?

If you weren't exposed to *Goodnight Moon* as a child, you might recognize how strange and fantastic the book actually is. Yes, that old lady is really a gigantic rabbit, there's a feral mouse on the loose, and the soon-to-be-slumbering little one has easy access to fireplace pokers. Look closely, and you'll discover further oddities: the books on the shelves change from page to page; someone steals the drying socks off the rack; the mailbox in the painting of the cow jumping over the moon sometimes disappears. Yet, for young readers, the story takes on a surreal coherence. The soothing colors and sweet couplets settle children into a state of drowsy acceptance. It is no surprise that *The New Yorker*, reviewing *Goodnight Moon* on its initial publication, described it as "hypnotic." Is that rabbit really an old lady? Well, say it enough times, and it becomes so.

A similar process happened during the past eight years. Under Bush, the nation we thought we knew was distorted into something almost unrecognizable, leaving us feeling strangely out of place in our own home—America.

Goodnight Moon reassured us that familiar things were intact, that everything was as it should be; if we could just lie back and obey the old lady's counsel, all would be well. The bedtime stories we got from the Bush administration had the same seductive aura of reassurance, the same promise of security. But, in fact, the great green room of *Goodnight Moon* was a danger zone. As noted in an op-ed piece in the *New York Times* a few years ago, the balloon presents a possible choking hazard, the bookshelf is unanchored to the wall, the fireplace has no screen. *Goodnight Moon* showed that if you can successfully lull someone into happily accepting the possibility that rabbits wear clothes but bears in chairs don't, you can probably convince them to accept just about anything.

So let us bid sweet dreams to Bush and his playmates Uncle Dick, Rummy, Condi, Brownie, Fredo, Hurricane Karen, Landslide, and Turd Blossom. Let's hope that they sleep for a long, long time.

Copyright © 2008 by Erich Origen and Gan Golan

Little, Brown and Company
Hachette Book Group USA
237 Park Avenue, New York, NY 10017
Visit our Web site at www.HachetteBookGroupUSA.com

First Edition: May 2008

Little, Brown and Company is a division of Hachette Book Group USA, Inc.
The Little, Brown logo is a trademark of Hachette Book Group USA, Inc.

ISBN 0-316-04041-X / 978-0-316-04041-9
LCCN 2008925069

10 9 8 7 6 5 4 3 2 1

RRD-IN

Printed in the United States of America